what's your excuse
for not being more
productive

what's your excuse ...

BEING MORE PRODUCTIVE?

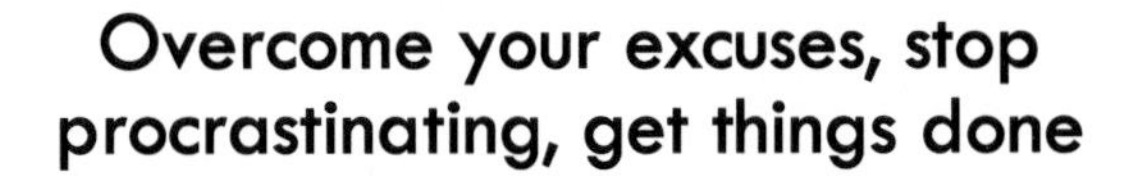

Overcome your excuses, stop procrastinating, get things done

juliet landau-pope

"If you've ever wondered why you get stuck, procrastinate or feel overwhelmed this book is for you. In this highly practical and insightful guide Juliet looks at the reasons behind our behaviour to offer a wealth of solutions for a more productive life"

Francesca Geens, productivity and technology strategist, Digital Dragonfly

"Finally, a book which helps us to understand the emotional components of why we procrastinate! Juliet's compassionate tone enables the reader to take an honest look at their behaviour, make strategic choices and live more productively with less stress"

Rivka Caroline, director, SoBeOrganized

"Juliet takes what could be a complicated topic and chops it into small, easy-to-digest bites that can each be read in under two minutes. You do have the time to get help from her!"

Helene Segura, author of The Inefficiency Assassin

"This is a very useful and easy-to-read book. It guides the reader, using lots of interesting anecdotes and quotes, to discover why it is that they individually procrastinate. Just don't put off buying it!"

Simon Michaelson, psychiatrist, CBT therapist and communication skills tutor

"You know what you need to do or what you want to do. But still, you just don't do it. Juliet's eminently practical book will help you lift the handbrake and accelerate into a brighter future"

John Barton, psychotherapist and counsellor

"Juliet offers a practical approach that has truly helped me change the way in which I think in order to become more productive. If you're a serial procrastinator, this book is for you. Escape the excuses and start doing whatever it is you need to do. It feels great!"

Lucinda Hutton, director, Nurturing Mums

"Juliet is a spirited and committed coach who absolutely knows how to get people unstuck"

John-Paul Flintoff, author, performer and journalist

"Juliet's warm and accessible writing style will inspire you to put down your to-do list and achieve even your least favourite task. She guides us past every obstacle to help us reach our goals. You will be inspired."

Rabbi Marcia Plumb

Also by this author

Clearing Your Clutter

Also in this series

Living a Life You Love
Getting Fit
Overcoming Stress
Being Better with Money
Loving Your Job
Eating Healthily
Being More Confident

What's Your Excuse for not Being More Productive?

This first edition published in 2017 by WYE Publishing
9 Evelyn Gardens, Richmond TW9 2PL
www.wyepublishing.com

ISBN 978-0-9956052-2-0

Cover and text design by Annette Peppis & Associates

www.whatsyourexcuse.co.uk
Follow What's Your Excuse…? on Twitter – @whats_yr_excuse
www.facebook.com/whatsyourexcusebooks

www.jlpcoach.com
Follow Juliet on Twitter – @jlpcoach

Printed and bound in Great Britain by
Marston Book Services Ltd, Oxfordshire

Contents

Introduction

How this book will help you

The deadline for completing your job application, essay or work presentation is fast approaching but you haven't yet made a start.

You compile endless to-do lists but never manage to tick more than a few items off.

You embark on important tasks but get too distracted to complete them.

Or maybe there's something you've always wanted to do but you've never been able to take the steps to achieve it.

If any of these scenarios sound familiar, you've experienced the perennial problem of procrastination. You may even be reading this book right now in order to avoid doing something more important!

You're not alone. Comedians joke about this. American TV host and writer Ellen de Generes says, 'Procrastinate now, don't put it off!' But if you're struggling to get more done at home, at work or in your studies you'll know that it's no laughing matter.

Throughout my career I've been fascinated by what holds people back and what drives them forward. My work as a lecturer, coach and professional organiser has involved countless conversations with people who are eager to be more productive but instead find themselves 'stuck'. From students grappling with academic assignments to business owners sorting out paperwork, from parents juggling domestic duties and professional responsibilities to elderly clients decluttering before they downsize, I hear the same question: 'Why can't I just crack on with the tasks I need to do?'

This book addresses the most common excuses I've heard over the years from clients. I've used some of them myself. While circumstances vary, excuses share similar themes. Many boil down to lack of clarity or confidence; all contribute to habits which form mental clutter – they build up imperceptibly over time, gradually become entrenched and then get in the way. For each excuse outlined in this book I invite you to explore an alternative perspective.

The advice in this book is very practical. If you're keen to make more effective use of your time and you're willing to question the way you perceive yourself, read on. I have plenty of ideas for you!

What does it mean to be productive?

From the nineteenth century the term 'productivity' has been used to evaluate the economic performance of farms, factories, companies and countries. It also features in discussions about human resources to assess the efficiency of groups or individuals in the workplace. In recent years however there's been a surge of interest in the idea of *personal* productivity. So what exactly does that mean?

Broadly speaking it means *getting things done*. David Allen, best-selling author and presenter of sell-out seminars with that very title, is one of the new wave of productivity experts, sharing time management strategies for professionals and business leaders.[1] But a growing number of coaches, consultants, trainers and educators believe that the idea of personal productivity is relevant beyond the workplace. Some focus on strategies for particular groups, often drawing on their own experience. Rivka Caroline, mother of seven and author of From Frazzled to Focused, offers practical

1 David Allen, Getting Things Done: the art of stress-free productivity, Piatkus, 2001

solutions for busy mums.[2] Helene Segura, aka the Inefficiency Assassin, shares time management lessons for stressed-out teachers and entrepreneurs.[3]

The advent of new technologies over the last decade has transformed the way we travel, work, shop, communicate, study and socialise. It's not only the changes to our lifestyle but the pace of those changes which can often lead to a sense of being overloaded and overwhelmed. The faster things change, the harder it is to keep up. So being productive can involve not only ticking off tasks on your to-do list but also feeling in control of your schedule.

It's not just what you accomplish at work, at home and in your studies, but also how you feel about your ability to shift habits which undermine happiness and wellbeing. In other words productivity is about making choices, taking action and creating positive changes in any aspect of your life.

---

2 Rivka Caroline, From Frazzled to Focused: The Ultimate Guide for Moms Who Want to Reclaim Their Time, Their Sanity and Their Lives, River Grove Books, 2013

3 Helene Segura, The Inefficiency Assassin: Time Management Tactics for Working Smarter, Not Longer, New World Library, 2016

Why we struggle to be productive

It was as an undergraduate that I first witnessed and experienced for myself the pressure to be productive. All-night essay crises were a regular feature of student life but no one talked about how they could be avoided. It wasn't until a few years later when I became a university lecturer myself that I realised how many colleagues were staying up late to mark the essays which students had struggled to submit on time.

Whilst teaching at the Open University I started to talk more openly with students about time management. Many were studying part-time and juggling other responsibilities. They often berated themselves for writing assignments just before (or sometimes after) deadlines. To learn more about motivation I undertook courses in sports psychology and educational management and then embarked on a training programme at CTI Coaches Training Institute to become a professional co-active coach. All of this training enhanced my understanding of self-limiting behaviour: the myriad ways in which we sabotage our own success through our beliefs, attitudes and perceptions. I don't underestimate barriers that arise from other problems – social inequalities for example – but I've learned to question some of the assumptions about what can and can't be changed.

Since launching my coaching and decluttering business, JLP Coach, in 2008 I've worked with hundreds of individuals from diverse backgrounds who were struggling to get through their to-do lists. Whenever I run training courses, speak at business networking events or lead workshops I meet busy people who are eager to be more productive. More often than not this quest is linked to a desire to avoid procrastination, a major source of stress among teenagers and adults alike.

So what is procrastination, and how does it affect productivity?

Broadly speaking I believe there are two types of procrastination. You might like to think about which resonates most with you:

- **Not leaving the starting block**
  You find umpteen ways to avoid an important task but the longer you delay it the harder it becomes to take the first step. It might lead to missing or postponing deadlines, or leaving things to the very last minute

- **Getting stuck**
  You launch into a task but then lose momentum, perhaps when you encounter an obstacle. As a result you slow down or maybe abandon the project altogether. This might become a pattern, leading to numerous unfinished projects that continue to haunt you

In both cases the problem can feel insurmountable. But the good news is that there are lots of simple and practical strategies that can help you to overcome procrastination.

The first step to changing behaviour is to acknowledge it. So where in your life are *you* stuck? Are you trying to be more productive in any of these areas of your life right now?

- Home – DIY projects, decluttering and paperwork, unpacking after a move
- Career – making decisions about new directions, completing job applications, applying for promotions, meeting deadlines
- Study – writing essays, preparing presentations, organising resources, revising for exams
- Relationships – starting or ending relationships, dating after a break-up, staying in touch with friends or family, broaching difficult conversations

- Health and wellbeing – making medical or dental appointments, starting an exercise regime, changing eating habits
- Money – dealing with debts, completing tax returns, making a will
- Hobbies and interests – writing, painting, crafting, practising a musical instrument, taking part in sports or leisure activities
- Community – joining a local group, getting involved with a campaign

What could you add to this list?

The price you pay when you're stuck

Sometimes the cost of inaction can be expressed in monetary terms. Failure to submit your tax return before the designated deadline, for example, results in hefty fines. But often the cost is your time. Many of the students I coach, from teenagers to mature students at university, confide that they can spend several hours per week finding ways to avoid essential academic tasks, which all add up to a colossal amount of wasted time.

Harder to calculate but equally demoralising are the emotional costs of procrastination, such as:

- Guilt
- Shame
- Frustration
- Anger
- Exasperation
- Embarrassment
- Fury
- Humiliation
- Despair

These feelings may also manifest themselves in physical

symptoms, affecting health and wellbeing.

And it's not only you who pays a price when you procrastinate. If you've ever been kept waiting by someone – a friend, relative or colleague – you'll appreciate the potential knock-on effects of procrastinating behaviour. Missing deadlines can mean letting other people down or causing them undue stress – your reputation and relationships subsequently suffer.

The good news

The positive side to all of this is that you're not alone. Procrastination is a universal feature of human behaviour. Regardless of nationality, culture, race or ethnicity procrastination knows no boundaries so you're in good company. Contrary to some popular beliefs it's not linked to intelligence nor to level of education. Much of the research in this field involves data drawn from students or academics but that may be because they're relatively easy for academics to survey.

There's also some evidence that procrastination diminishes with age but experts differ on why this happens. Is it due to increased awareness of mortality? As we get older, we become more aware that our time on earth is limited so this might propel us to get on with things. Or is it that we develop greater self-awareness and resilience that enable us to overcome obstacles to productivity?

And the impact of procrastination isn't always negative. While attention is diverted from the things you need to do there may even be some benefits. You may know from experience that when you're avoiding one particular task you might plough an inordinate amount of energy into another entirely different set of activities. Have you ever noticed that when it's time to get on with an important assignment or to write a report you suddenly develop an urge to clear out your desk or scrub the inside of the fridge? This has been referred to as 'productive procrastination'. So be assured that you're not lazy or ineffective, you're just putting your energies into the wrong things.

While a very small proportion of people suffer from chronic procrastination, I regard all procrastination as a habit rather than a character trait. Habits can be debilitating and destructive but the good news is that with motivation, encouragement and support habits can also be shifted.

What are excuses?

Being asked 'What's your excuse?' might feel a little uncomfortable. But my intention is not to judge or put you on the defensive. I am inviting you to explore the stories that you tell yourself. Excuses, I believe, are just stories that we construct to explain or validate the situations in which we find ourselves.

When life gets too complicated or hectic we can seek refuge in stories and that's when we're also more likely to get stuck. Historian Yuval Noah Harari explained in a recent interview:

> 'When we try to observe the world and when we try to observe ourselves, the mind constantly generates stories and fictions and explanations and imposes them on reality; and we cannot see what is really happening because we are blinded by the stories and fictions that we create, or that other people create and we believe'[4]

There may well be an element of truth behind an excuse but it's still only one perspective. An excuse can become

---

4 *Andrew Anthony, Yuval Noah Hariri: homo sapiens, as we know them, will disappear in a century or two, The Guardian, 19 March 2017*

a limiting belief if it's not challenged.

The key to boosting motivation and productivity is therefore to explore different perspectives and find ways to shift the story as well as the habit. And when a shift happens the results can be extraordinary.

How to use this book

This book addresses the most common excuses that my clients express to people around them and, more importantly, to themselves. As you read through them, reflect on the ones which resonate most with you: those which you have used in the past and those which you might be using now in response to current challenges.

Throughout the book I'll ask questions to uncover your beliefs about yourself and the tasks you're struggling with.

Like any story an excuse can be reframed and retold in any number of ways, but what I'll encourage you to do is:

- Notice what you are doing (as well as what you are not doing)
- Let go of self-judgment
- Shift your story by reframing it or reviewing the underlying assumptions

I'll be asking you to listen to the words you use to explain your inaction: the excuses that you make to your partner, your colleagues, your boss or yourself.

But don't limit your inquiry into those excuses. Get curious, probe deeper, consider alternative or additional explanations and see how they resonate. One thing to notice about the excuses examined in this book is that they are often inter-dependent: if you feel too busy, you'll worry about not having time and if you're overwhelmed, you probably won't know where to start. And one excuse can very often mask another, perhaps less palatable one.

Feel free to dip into sections of this book which strike you as particularly relevant. Or select pages at random and be open to whatever ideas you encounter.

Enjoy!

The Excuses

Time

I don't have time

I once saw an advert in a cartoon with the slogan 'Every Mum's Dream', for a watch which displayed twenty-five hours. Aside from the sexist stereotype (I'm sure plenty of dads also hanker after an extra sixty minutes in a day) it highlighted a common malaise.

Lack of time is one of the most common excuses for putting off the things we claim we want to do, like learning a new language or planning a holiday. It also applies to things we feel we 'should' be doing such as going to the gym or dealing with personal finances.

Thanks to this common complaint time management has become not only a buzzword but also an industry. It's a phrase used to sell a growing range of products and services from stationery to seminars and podcasts to planners, all of which give the impression that somehow time can be tamed.

The harsh reality is that time isn't malleable and it simply can't be managed. Despite all the science fiction fantasies, no one's yet invented the technology to make time stretch, slow down or stop. And for each and every one of us on the planet, there are just twenty-four hours in a day.

Author H Jackson Browne says:

> 'Don't say you don't have enough time. You have exactly the same number of hours per day that were given to Helen Keller, Louis Pasteur, Michelangelo, Mother Teresa, Leonardo da Vinci, Thomas Jefferson, and Albert Einstein'[5]

Instead of focusing on time management we need to refocus the conversation to talk about *self*-management. And at the core of this conversation should be questions about decisions and the factors that influence those decisions.

> We need to refocus the conversation to talk about *self*-management

Yes, our lives are curtailed by circumstances that make huge demands on our time: health, relationships, careers, community. They all impact on time. But we can make some choices and even small shifts can make a huge difference.

So how can you start to make more effective use of your time?

Many productivity experts advocate an audit, using paper or digital tools such as charts or apps. This creates

5 H Jackson Browne, Life's Little Instruction Book, Rutledge Hill Press, 1991

a snapshot of your schedule and helps to identify patterns of behaviour. This can be useful as a monitoring exercise but I'm not convinced it motivates change. For some of my clients completing forms and recording detailed time logs can add to their stress, so as a coach my approach is slightly different. I don't advocate any one specific system. Rather than telling you what to do, I'm more interested in finding out how you feel about the demands and duties which are currently filling up the space in your schedule. This helps to demonstrate the notion of choice – what you opt to hold onto and what you're willing to let go.

I'm also fascinated by the concept of *time clutter* – surplus 'stuff' which accumulates just like books and clothes; tasks which once served a purpose but are now in the way, preventing us from doing what we really want to do or being who we want to be. The key to decluttering your diary is to focus on what matters most. So instead of bemoaning a lack of time, define your priorities.

It can take patience and persistence (and sometimes professional help) to connect with core values and identify your priorities. And of course they will change through different periods of your life. But it's a worthwhile investment because there really isn't any other way to ensure that you make the most of the limited time available. As Stephen Covey, author of

The 7 Habits of Highly Effective People, says, 'The main thing is to keep the main thing the main thing'.[6]

Now when you're caught up with the demands of a busy schedule it's easy to lose sight of the 'main thing'. It's worth pausing periodically to consider which aspects of your life are most meaningful. What do you value most? Try to build this type of inquiry into a routine: on Sunday evenings, when you survey the week ahead, decide on your priorities for the week and plan accordingly.

Another strategy is to take a few moments to reflect on the future. Fast forward in your mind to a point in time that feels quite distant, perhaps ten or twenty years into the future. Picture yourself at that later stage in life, surveying the past. What would you like to have accomplished? What would you like to be most proud of? And when your life is over what legacy would you like to have left? How would you most wish to be remembered?

This exercise can help you to prioritise. After all, time can't be managed but it can be allocated more purposefully.

---

6 *Stephen Covey, The 7 Habits of Highly Effective People, Free Press, 1989*

I'm too busy

Do you rush from one meeting to another or schedule activities to fill every minute of the day? Are you so busy doing things that you feel you should be doing that you don't have time for the things you actually want to do?

Eavesdrop on any conversation nowadays, in playgrounds or pubs, staff rooms or supermarkets, and you're likely to hear people competing over how busy they are. At networking events entrepreneurs engage in 'busy bravado' as if it would be shameful to own up to having some spare time. Meanwhile parents, especially those who juggle work and childcare, persist in presenting themselves as constantly on the go. But when and, more importantly, *why* did being busy become a badge of honour?

Why did being busy become a badge of honour?

So first of all ask yourself if you are genuinely too busy or if it's just that you've been caught up in the modern fixation with busy-ness.

Despite technological advances and economic improvements life doesn't seem to be getting any simpler. On the contrary, even the most affluent people can be money-rich but still time-poor.

In a TED talk entitled 'In Praise of Slowness' Carl

Honoré describes contemporary society as 'marinated in the culture of speed'.[7] He talks about people rushing about, cramming more and more into their schedule, and how this obsession with busy-ness takes a toll on health and relationships as well as productivity. But this observation isn't entirely new. Ancient philosophers also grappled with the problem of trying to do too much. Socrates is reputed to have warned, 'Beware the barrenness of a busy life'.

If you're blaming a busy lifestyle for neglecting people or projects try decluttering your diary. This means removing unnecessary commitments and making time for what matters most. And most importantly it means abandoning the idea that being busy makes one a better person.

Here's how to do it:

- **Review your diary**
  Take a step back and try to examine your schedule impartially and without judgement. Notice what you're doing on a daily basis. What is making you so busy? How do you spend your most valuable resource – time?
- **Prioritise**

---

7 Carl Honoré, In Praise of Slowness, TED talk, 2005: https://www.ted.com/talks/carl_honore_praises_slowness/transcript?language=en#t-290000

You may have heard the expression, 'When everything is important, nothing is'. It's particularly relevant to being productive. Unless you define clear priorities and use them to organise yourself you'll never escape the busy trap. Identify your most important tasks and do them first

- **Learn to say No**
  Discover the positive power of the word 'No'. If you need to set boundaries with friends, family or colleagues it's a small but incredibly effective tool. If you find that awkward you may need to practise using it, preferably without apologising. You don't have to say yes to everything!

And finally, try dropping the busy banner by substituting the word 'active'. The next time someone asks if you're busy at work or at home tell them instead that you're active. It comes across as a little less frenetic and will remind you that you're in control.

You might also want to read the "I don't have time" chapter if you haven't already done so and "It's not my job" for more on how to say No.

I suffer from FOMO

Do you overcommit and find yourself too busy for Fear Of Missing Out? Added to the Oxford English Dictionary in 2013, the term FOMO defines a particularly modern anxiety, usually fuelled by social media, which gives the impression that other people are having more fun or living their lives more fully than you.

On a rational level we know that social media presents a distorted view of the world and that people are highly selective about the images and updates they share. Nonetheless it contributes to unhealthy social pressure and competition. Why stay at home to complete your tax return or revise for exams when your friends are going out on the town?

If the pace of your life is becoming too frenetic consider how FOMO might be undermining your resolve or your confidence and reassure yourself that you can cope with 'missing out' sometimes. Question the assumptions that you're making about having to be included in things and remind yourself that the consequences of not being included are unlikely to be dire. An event may seem tempting but is it really a once-in-a-lifetime opportunity? There will almost

There will almost certainly be other possibilities in the future certainly be other possibilities in the future: that band will tour again, your friends will arrange other meet-ups, that film will be screened for weeks.

So tackle your FOMO by accepting that you simply can't (and don't need to) do everything. Flex that decision-making muscle, learn to make active choices about how you spend your time and recognise that the quality of experiences matters more than quantity.

I don't have the block of time I need

Are you avoiding a major task because you don't have a sizeable enough block of time to dedicate to it? You might want to clear out the shed but don't have an entire day to tackle it, or maybe you want to research holiday destinations but don't have the couple of hours required to spend online.

Our schedules are so packed that there are only two possible solutions:

- Don't wait for time, make it. Carve out the space in your schedule, even if it requires planning well ahead
- Instead of doing it all in one go, make use of smaller

chunks of time to tackle it. This isn't the same as multi-tasking – I'm not suggesting you try to juggle different activities at the same time. I do believe, however, that it's worth using pockets of time, however small, to start or progress things that we want to do

When your goal is clear and your mind is focused it's extraordinary what you can accomplish in a very short burst. In response to a challenge from a close friend Keats reportedly wrote his classic poem 'On the Cricket and the Grasshopper' in just fifteen minutes.

I invite clients who procrastinate about decluttering to see how much stuff they can get through in just ten or fifteen minutes, which is enough time to fill a bag with unwanted clothes or papers but not long enough to get bored. Similarly, students revising for exams can be encouraged to learn a short list of vocabulary or practise writing an essay plan in a short period of time.

When you know that time is severely limited, you can often work quickly and efficiently. The key is to have a clear purpose and to define a micro-goal. This doesn't have to be overly ambitious. Small acts can make a huge difference and add up to larger ones.

I still have plenty of time

If you perceive a deadline as distant there's little incentive to get started. If your presentation is due next month it can seem like an eternity away. Yes, on a rational level, it makes sense to start the research today, work at a leisurely pace and complete it well in advance but you find yourself putting it aside and waiting until the deadline feels more urgent.

Various studies have shown that perception of time plays a key role in motivation. Researchers at the University of Chicago asked two groups of students to complete a four hour task within a four-day period. Those who were assigned the job on the 26th April and asked to finish by the end of April were more likely to start sooner than those given the job a few days later with a deadline in the first week of May. The change of month made students feel that the task was less urgent.[8]

Research by Neil Lewis and Daphna Oyserman also shows that the way in which numbers are presented has a significant impact on our perception of time.[9] When

---

8 Yanping Tu and Dilip Soman, The Categorization of Time and Its Impact on Task Initiation, Journal of Consumer Research, August 2014

9 Neil Lewis and Daphna Oyserman, When Does the Future Begin? Time Metrics Matter, Connecting Present and Future Selves, Psychological Science, April 2015

deadlines are expressed in smaller units of measurement, say days rather than weeks, people imagine the deadline to be closer. So adjusting these 'time metrics' can have a profound effect on motivation.

Adjusting these 'time metrics' can have a profound effect on motivation

So how to boost motivation when there's no obvious pressure? Instead of thinking about your deadline as two weeks away, try saying it's due in fourteen days. Then consider how many of those days you'll have access to the library or your office. If you'd like to take the weekends off that leaves just ten working days. During this period you'll also have other commitments which will take up time. Make a list of these – not just work commitments but personal ones too. Does that alter your perception of the time you have available before a deadline? You might start to think about how little time you have left rather than how much, and hopefully this will help to kick-start you into action.

I'll do it someday....

As I say to my coaching clients, 'someday' isn't a day of the week. If you're genuinely committed to something there are only two options:

- Fix a date to do it, write it in your diary and ideally tell someone else so that you'll be accountable
- Do it now!

Knowledge

I don't know what to do

Tackling something for the first time can be daunting, especially when you don't fully understand what the task involves. The more complex a project is, the more difficult it can be to work out exactly what you need to do. And lack of clarity fuels all kinds of other uncertainties.

In some instances you might be intimidated by the scope of a project or by the new tools or skills required. Figuring out what needs to be done might involve going back to basics to define specific goals. This might require you to check instructions or consult others. Most importantly, it means coming to terms with *conscious incompetence*[10] – acknowledging the limits of your own understanding. If knowledge is power, then *self*-knowledge is key to motivation.

Get clear on what you need to know and let go of any embarrassment about not yet having the skills or knowledge that you need to get unstuck.

---

10 For more information about unconscious incompetence and how it fits into the four stages of learning see Linda Gordon's article 'Learning a New Skill is Easier Said than Done' athttp://www.gordontraining.com/free-workplace-articles/learning-a-new-skill-is-easier-said-than-done

Have you defined the different steps that you need to take? Are you aware of relevant rules, regulations or conventions? And if not, how can you find out? Put bluntly, if you don't know what to do, you need to find out!

Here's an example:

LK was in her first year at a prestigious university. She had achieved excellent A Level results but was finding it difficult to focus on her assignments. When it came to producing essays she spent far too long researching topics or making copious notes. As a result she had little time to draft and edit her essay and found herself either missing deadlines or staying up all night writing and handing in the work at the very last minute.

LK found her course interesting and compared to her peers she spent more time in the library and at her desk but she was berating herself for not being productive. 'I put in the hours but I don't know why it takes me so long to get around to writing', she told me. Through coaching it became clear that the crux of the matter for LK was that she didn't feel confident about what writing essays at university level entailed. At school she had been given clear guidelines but now that she was expected to study more independently she felt very uncertain.

The challenge for LK was to acknowledge that she didn't know what to do. The process of writing a university assignment was unlike anything she had undertaken at school. Her procrastination wasn't due to laziness or stupidity; it was due to confusion about what the task entailed. Clarifying this issue made all the difference and LK was able to ask her tutors for the guidance she needed.

So if you're avoiding something that you haven't attempted before, go back to basics and ask yourself if you know what you're expected to do. And if you don't, find out. Consult with others if necessary to clarify what exactly the task requires you to do.

I need more information

We live in an information age, dominated by digital devices that offer instant access to unlimited amounts of data. But when it comes to productivity, the need to research or a perceived lack of information is one of the most common causes of getting stuck.

In days gone by academic research involved visiting libraries, sometimes sifting through card catalogues and ordering up written materials from a mysterious place called the 'stacks'. At the British Library, for example, this process could take hours, sometimes even days. Nowadays, we can access books, journals and newspapers within seconds by tapping on our keyboards or surfing on our smart phones.

The downside is that we can fall all too easily into an endless quest for more and more facts or ideas, and this applies to almost any aspect of our lives. Whether you're teaching or learning, job-hunting or shopping, online research opens up endless opportunities to investigate. But as one link leads to another, you can stray further from the tasks you need to tackle. Even mundane errands such as booking a train ticket can become excessively time-consuming because of the number of websites to check and the variety of options to investigate. And while you're engaged in these explorations, you're likely to be neglecting other important or urgent projects.

If you recognise this behaviour, ask yourself whether research has become a pretext for procrastination. Try answering the following questions:

- What exactly do you need to know? Have you defined the parameters of your research?
- How much background information and detail do you really need?
- How many options/case studies do you need to explore?
- How will you know when you've done enough?
- Where's the best place to get your information?

Do you really need to spend hours online or is there someone you could consult instead?

Define the parameters of your fact-finding. Set a deadline and accept that whatever you've learned about the subject by that time will be sufficient. If you're preparing an assignment, for example, commit to start writing. You can always return to the research at a later date but you need to move forward.

I don't know where to start

If you're overwhelmed by the scope of a project you might be hesitating because there's no obvious place to begin.

Perhaps you're worried that there is, objectively speaking, a correct place to start and that a misjudgement could have dire consequences.

An event to organise, a room to clear, a book to write – if you're faced with a complex set of tasks, you may struggle to put them in order. Picking one thing to do first can be a tough decision. But once you do make that move you'll be on your way.

Here are some ideas to help you decide where to start:

- Map it out. Take time to identify the different tasks then create a plan. Once you've done this the starting point might be more obvious
- Question your assumptions. For instance, you don't necessarily need to write an introduction first or compile a report by writing up events in the order that they took place. The content may need to be chronological but you can write up different sections in any order you choose
- Start somewhere that won't be too demanding. Treat it as a gentle warm-up. Tackle an element of the project that doesn't represent too much of a challenge. Engage gradually and feel your confidence and your competence grow
- Or completely ignore the previous suggestion and take Brian Tracy's advice instead: *Eat That Frog!* Tracy recommends tackling the most unpleasant tasks first, ideally first thing in the morning.[11] You'll be motivated by the sense of achievement, and from then on your day can only get better

It may not matter where you begin; anywhere is better than remaining stuck. The first step may be the most difficult but try not to agonise about it. And once you do get started, don't look back!

---

11 Brian Tracy, Eat That Frog! Hodder & Stoughton, 2001

I don't know what I want

In 2008 when I set up my coaching and decluttering business everyone I spoke to asked if I had a website. I felt under immense pressure to establish an online presence, not only to attract clients but also to establish credibility. However, it took me over two years to launch my first website primarily because I couldn't decide what I wanted. The challenge wasn't technical – I was ready to outsource the design and building of the website. The issue was conceptual – I didn't have clarity in terms of business goals. As a result it was impossible to reach any decisions about branding, marketing, design, etc.

Confusion about my new professional identity was holding me up. I couldn't move forward with commissioning the website until I'd made a number of decisions. I didn't know what message I wanted the website to project because I hadn't yet defined what the business was about.

Back then it was still possible for someone to start trading without a website. I found clients and they found me through face-to-face networking, live events and personal referrals. But within a couple of years it became harder to postpone. Eventually I realised that the price I was paying for *not* having a website was higher than the risk of making the 'wrong' choices.

Working with a coach helped me to crystallise my

thoughts and formulate a business plan. This enabled me to make a number of decisions about what I wanted to express through my website. It also helped me come to terms with the fact that any form of marketing, online or in print, could be changed. So even if I wasn't certain about one element – how often to run workshops, for example – the details could be updated at any time.

Indecision can sometimes be linked to overthinking

Indecision can sometimes be linked to overthinking. When you're dazzled by the details or bamboozled by choice, you might prefer to avoid or postpone a decision. This phenomenon is sometimes called *analysis paralysis*. One way out of this condition is to differentiate between the more important decisions and those which matter less. Focusing on what matters most can put things in perspective and help you move forward.

The stress of delaying a decision can be worse than any possible outcome. In other words, any decision can be better than none. If you don't know what you do want, try focusing on what you *don't* want. It can be helpful to narrow choices by eliminating options.

Another way to develop decision-making skills is to notice and celebrate the decisions that you do make on a daily basis. Whether it's picking an outfit to wear in the morning or navigating a new cycling route to work, pay more attention to the positive and active choices that you make. This will help you to feel more capable of moving forward when you're grounded by indecision.

Mood

I'm overwhelmed

If I had to name the most common feeling expressed by my clients I'd sum it up in one word: *overwhelmed*.

Some describe it as feeling paralysed, unable to move in any direction. Others use words which reflect fear and anxiety: drowning, sinking, capsizing. The word has nautical origins – when a boat is overwhelmed, water is spilling over the sides and disaster seems inevitable. A feeling of being overwhelmed is a symptom of catastrophizing, of perceiving a problem to be insurmountable.

When there are so many emails in your inbox that you don't know where to start or too many boxes to unpack after moving home, it's tempting to avoid them altogether. How can you take charge, regain control of a situation that feels daunting or doomed? In essence the challenge is how to move from overwhelm to 'at the helm'.

Among the most overwhelming situations are life events that involve major disruptions, either practical or emotional: bereavement, divorce, moving home or having a baby. Many of the people who contact me for help with decluttering and organising are also dealing with these sorts of transitions, which exacerbate the problem.

Feeling overwhelmed can also stem from trying to do too many things at the same time. Contrary to popular belief multi-tasking isn't the most effective way of getting things done and the effects can be damaging to health as well as productivity. Recent studies by neurologist Earl Miller show that repeatedly switching attention from one activity to another can be exhausting because it takes time to regain your focus.[12] So resist the temptation to embark on several tasks simultaneously.

Resist the temptation to embark on several tasks simultaneously

When you're overwhelmed, the antidote may feel counter-intuitive: *do nothing.* Stop, breathe, regroup. Find somewhere quiet to sit for a few moments, close your eyes and take a few deep breaths. You don't need to sit cross-legged on a yoga mat to do this. Simply carving out a few seconds of your day to concentrate on the here and now can help to restore some form of equilibrium. And when you're feeling calmer, you'll

---

12 Earl Miller, Why You Shouldn't Multitask, http://fortune.com/2016/12/07/why-you-shouldnt-multitask

be in a better frame of mind to move from inaction to action.

I witnessed a different version of this strategy among Russian friends. Whenever they left their home they would put on their coats, gather up their bags and then sit down together at the kitchen table for a couple of minutes before going out. According to Russian custom either good or bad spirits accompany you on a trip so it's a good omen to sit quietly rather than rush out. Even if you're alone, it helps to gather your thoughts and take a moment to breathe. Whatever your beliefs, try it and see.

You might also find it helpful to write down all the things you need to do. Committing your thoughts to paper (or screen) might enable you to unburden your mind. Talking to someone else – a friend, relative or professional – can help you to think more clearly. It's only by taking time to declutter your mind that you can decide where to focus time and attention.

I just don't feel like it

There's a flat-packed bookshelf in your hall waiting to be assembled but you'd rather be reading the weekend papers. Or you need to look for some important documents but feel a sudden yen to take the dog for a walk. This excuse might be hard to admit to because it sounds rather self-indulgent: are you procrastinating because you simply don't have any inclination to do what you need to do?

If you don't feel like tackling something, explore your ambivalence: start by asking yourself whether the task actually *needs* to be done. Do you really need more bookshelves? Is it essential to find those missing papers? If the answer is 'yes', then consider whether you're the only person who can do it. Can you reduce your to-do list by either deleting the task or delegating to others? (See "Only I can do this" for more on delegation).

Lack of motivation can be a source and a symptom of anxiety, particularly where a task seems too daunting or where the purpose isn't clear. But if the job in question is a recurring task, consider how you can create a habit. Successful athletes don't wait until they 'feel like' practising their game. They develop rigorous training schedules to mobilise themselves, come rain or shine. Personal whim is irrelevant. Sports psychologists also believe in the importance of setting goals and monitoring performance on a routine basis.

Consider how you can create a habit

Planning, preparing and being accountable to someone else, such as a colleague or coach, also diminishes the risk of letting your mood undermine your motivation. Put simply, when you tell someone that you'll do something, you're more likely to make it happen.

The words you use when you tell people (and indeed yourself) what you intend to do are important. Don't announce what you *want*, *need* or *hope* to do: those words express desire or duty but not commitment. State instead what you *will* do. It's a braver but simple way of convincing yourself that you will indeed step up to the challenge. The shift might seem subtle but it makes a difference. The words 'I will' convey firm intention. Think of it as putting a stake in the ground.

Similarly, don't hedge your bets by suggesting that you'll merely *try* to start or finish something; demonstrate resolve and boost your own confidence by saying 'I will'. These tweaks are more than linguistic tricks; they're strategies to create a more positive and purposeful mindset.

I'm too tired

If your eyelids droop as you scroll through emails after lunch, you'll know how difficult it is to concentrate when you're tired. It's not unusual to experience dips in energy throughout the day. Studies in neuroscience prove what we know from experience about circadian rhythms, which are the levels of wakefulness which rise and fall in patterns over a twenty-four hour period.[13] Understanding your own body clock and understanding when you're most able to concentrate and then organising your day accordingly is a sure-fire way to boost productivity.

Tiredness (along with headaches and being unable to concentrate) can also be a symptom of dehydration. Our bodies contain a high proportion of water so need a steady intake of water to function well. This is especially important for students while preparing for exams because revision is so demanding, physically and mentally.

Caffeine might appeal as a quick-fix stimulant but it can make dehydration worse because of its diuretic effects. Also beware of so-called 'energy drinks' – these might provide a short-lived jolt because of high levels of sugar and caffeine but experts warn about the harmful effects of these drinks as well as the risk of addiction.[14] The best option to combat dehydration is to just drink water. For this reason I always advise clients to keep

---

13 Nuffield Department of Clinical Sciences, University of Oxford, https://www.ndcn.ox.ac.uk/research/sleep-circadian-neuroscience-institute

10 Frontiers in Public Health, Energy Drink Consumption in Europe http://journal.frontiersin.org/article/10.3389/fpubh.2014.00134/full, 2014

a glass or bottle of water handy in order to ward off fatigue.

> Don't be tempted to jeopardise your health

The growing use among students of 'smart drugs', also known as nootropics, is also concerning because of dangerous side-effects.[15] Don't be tempted to jeopardise your health with these.

Ultimately, the only solution for tiredness is to get more sleep. In an interview for Business Insider, Arianna Huffington, founder of the Huffington Post, says that we are witnessing unprecedented levels of sleep deprivation these days which undermine creativity, efficiency and wellbeing. A self-styled 'sleep evangelist', Huffington is on a mission to raise awareness of the value of napping. She even believes that employees should be allowed to take naps at work:

> 'In the next few years nap rooms are going to be as universal as conference rooms, because the science now is conclusive about the value of napping. Do you want exhausted employees being exhausted during the day, or do you want them to go have a twenty minute nap

---

15 *Lucas Fothergill, Study drugs: are Modafinil, Noopept and Nootropics essential in helping students on the road to exams? The Independent, 7 December 2015*

> and literally have another day ahead of them? Because that's how restorative a nap is'[16]

Even if you can't fall asleep, your mind and body will still benefit and Huffington suggests that to gain maximum benefit, you should build naps into your daily routine. As with other strategies to improve productivity, creating and sustaining this healthy habit can make all the difference.

One final thought on tiredness: putting things off can feel exhausting. So take a look at some of the other advice in this book for ideas on getting things done. Ticking something off your to-do list might actually have an energising effect.

I'm not ready

You've been talking for years about moving house or travelling somewhere special but whenever anyone asks how your plans are progressing you tell them you're not ready. What's holding you up? Can you say with

---

16 Rachel Gillet, From napping at work to clearing your mind before bed http://uk.businessinsider.com/arianna-huffington-answers-all-your-questions-about-sleep-2016-4?r=US&IR=T/#-8

certainty that the time is not right? Or is it that you simply don't feel ready?

Are you waiting for something outside of your control to change, such as the weather to improve or the price of houses to fall? Or are you awaiting a particular milestone such as a special birthday? You might associate readiness with a specific age or stage of life such as parenthood or retirement. Or is it merely your mood that needs to shift?

Is it merely your mood that needs to shift?

The following questions might help you to clarify what readiness is:

- Are you waiting for something specific to happen? Do you need someone else to make a decision or take some action? If so, take a look at "Someone else is holding me up"
- Do you need more resources such as information, funding or support? Compile a checklist and analyse what you need to do in order to get these
- Do you have clear and specific standards to measure your readiness and monitor your progress towards it? For example, if your goal is to run a marathon, you won't feel ready until you can cover a certain distance

The bottom line is: what will it take for you to feel ready? What will readiness look and feel like? How will you know that you're ready? What is absolutely necessary for you to be ready and what is merely desirable?

Ivan Turgenev wrote, 'If we wait for the moment when everything, absolutely everything, is ready, we shall never begin'.[17] Planning and preparation may be essential but at a certain point you just need to take action. This might be akin to leaping off a diving board or it could be a small shuffle in the right direction. You may never feel completely sure of the outcome but you can be ready to trust in yourself and others involved in the project.

At a certain point you just need to take action

Hugh Laurie, award-winning actor, writer, comedian and musician said of his illustrious career: 'It's a terrible thing, I think, to wait until you're ready.... Actually, no one is ever ready to do anything. There is almost no such thing as ready. There is only now'.[18]

---

17 *Ivan Turgenev, First Love, Oxford Paperbacks, 1989*
18 *Sophie Harris, Hugh Laurie Sings the Blues, TimeOut, 2012*

Tasks

It's too boring

What are the most mind-numbing, soul-destroying, tiresome and tedious tasks you can think of? Chances are they include routine but vital tasks that you'll make every effort to avoid.

So how can we overcome our aversion to tackling boring tasks?

Some of the most useful research in this field comes from experts who support people with Attention Deficit Disorder (ADD) or Attention Deficit and Hyperactivity Disorder (ADHD) which both include a low boredom threshold. Sufferers who have learned to live and thrive with these conditions have much to teach us about motivation in the face of monotony. Strategies they use to beat boredom include developing routines, dividing projects into bite-sized chunks and limiting the time spent on any one task.

Let's consider how this could be applied to paperwork, one of the most common forms of clutter. When I started working as a professional organiser I discovered that there were two categories of people in the world: those who open their post every day and those (like many of my clients) who abandon it in piles, usually because it seems too tedious to deal with.

If you get into the habit of opening your post every day and putting junk mail straight into a recycling box it will be easier to manage because it will never build up into an intimidating pile and will be less boring as it will never become a big job.

Set a timer for a short period of time and see how much you can get done

Another option is to set a timer for a short period of time and see how much you can get done in that time. How many envelopes can you open? Can you dispose of all the unwanted catalogues, free newspapers and flyers during that time? A timer can boost productivity in two ways: first, it limits the time available to get bored, perhaps making it easier to endure. And second, it enables you to compete against yourself. Can you beat your own personal record of opening envelopes, discarding catalogues or clearing paper clutter in your hallway?

Sarah Bickers of Free Your Space is a professional organiser who works with people with ADHD.[19] She told me recently:

---

19 www.freeyourspace.com

> 'If you keep putting off getting started with a job, just set a kitchen timer for twenty minutes and commit to working at your task for that long. This creates a deadline and a visual display of time moving on. Often once you've started you'll decide to continue for longer, but either way you've started!'

Finally, consider this: although boredom gets bad press, experts in education believe it has positive aspects. Teresa Belton describes it as a source of creativity and innovation: it's through daydreaming and switching off that we give our imagination room to flourish.[20] Children subjected to a whirlwind calendar of extra-curricular activities are missing out on vital opportunities to experience boredom by not being allowed any downtime.

This has relevance for adults, too. Mundane activities can provide much-needed respite from over-stimulation. If you're putting off doing something mindless – like mowing the lawn or cleaning out the fridge – think about the project as a welcome interlude. As Jon Kabat-Zinn said in an interview for the Washington Post, 'When you pay attention to boredom

---

20 Teresa Belton, How Kids Can Benefit from Boredom, 23 September, 2013: http://theconversation.com/how-kids-can-benefit-from-boredom-65596

it gets unbelievably interesting'.[21]

Perhaps this fascination with boredom explains the sell-out popularity of the annual Boring Conference, now in its seventh year, which features speakers on topics ranging from 'the mundane, the ordinary, the obvious and the overlooked.'[22]

There's no point

How often do you stare into a messy playroom full of toys or a desk piled with papers and wonder if there is any point clearing it up because you know that within no time at all, the mess will simply reappear? Or maybe you're dealing with an overloaded inbox but know that as soon as you clear it out, there'll be another deluge. Why bother? It's hard to feel motivated when you don't expect your efforts to have any lasting impact.

Avoiding domestic duties can give rise to tensions among household members, especially between partners caught up in 'chore wars'. Many of the issues which couples in the UK argue about most frequently relate to chores which need to be tackled regularly

---

21 Cecilia Capuzzi Simon, Mr Mindfulness, Washington Post, July 2005

22 Boring Conference, https://boringconference.com

and of which the benefits are short-lived. For example, almost a third of couples admit to arguing about who changes bed linen. Another major source of contention is turning off lights![23]

So how can you find purpose in the repetitive tasks which provide little satisfaction because they are so easily undone?

The mythical Greek figure of Sisyphus is condemned by the gods to push a heavy boulder to the top of a mountain over and over again. No sooner does he reach the peak than the boulder rolls all the way down again. Yet, according to philosopher Albert Camus, futility need not give rise to despair.[24] As Sisyphus descends the mountain, aware of the absurdity of the situation, he is momentarily free. The future may look bleak and the past miserable but he finds a sense of purpose in the present. By contemplating the meaning of his existence he can even experience that most elusive emotion, happiness.

Can existential philosophy teach us anything about dealing with an ever-flowing laundry basket or a relentless stream of emails? Perhaps it encourages us to accept the limits to what we can control. Yes, washing

---

23 I've written for The Huffington Post about this – read my article at this address - http://www.huffingtonpost.co.uk/juliet-landaupope/powering-a-peaceful-home_b_15635182.html

24 Albert Camus, The Myth of Sisyphus, Penguin Great Ideas, 2005

clothes is boring and dealing with emails is mundane but railing against tasks won't stem the flow. If you can't see the point, you may be looking in the wrong place – it's not the result that matters but the process. Like Sisyphus, celebrate moments of freedom in between small tasks. Notice the improvements that you're making today and try not to dwell on the fact that your work may all be undone tomorrow.

It's too difficult

Think of something practical you've learned to do. Do you remember how you felt before you passed your driving test, learned to converse in Italian or acquired your first hundred followers on Twitter? You knew that it would take considerable practise and persistence but were prepared to give it a go. What spurred you to attempt it? How did you rise to the challenge? And what kept you on track when you encountered setbacks?

Research by Stanford psychologist Carol Dwek about how brains work has made a huge impact in classrooms, colleges and corporate training, and her ideas can also help you to deal with your own greatest obstacle, namely your mindset.[25] She identifies two mindsets:

- A **fixed** mindset is the belief that you have innate abilities, that your 'brain power' is limited and determined. If you hear a child say, 'I'm rubbish at maths', they're expressing a fixed mindset
- A **growth** mindset recognises the capacity of the brain to create new pathways and connections which enable us to learn and to grow. It's an exciting concept, supported by research from neuroscience

An experiment conducted with school children and then replicated among university students showed a clear pattern. A class was divided into two groups and each group was presented with one of the above explanations of how their brains functioned. Those who were told about the growth mindset not only performed better in tests but also enjoyed the tests more and even volunteered to take harder tests. They demonstrated motivation to learn despite any difficulties they encountered.

Like the child who believes that they simply can't do maths do you avoid tasks that you think you will find too difficult? Maybe you believe that 'you can't teach

---

25 Carol Dwek, Mindset: the new psychology of success, Random House, 2016

an old dog new tricks'? Long before Dweck explained the science, animal trainers had already debunked this myth! But just because you can't do something now doesn't mean you can't learn.

Here's an example from one of my coaching clients:

LM set up her own business as a massage therapist and within a year she had built up a solid client base. While she loved working with clients, she avoided bookkeeping and other administrative tasks. She wasn't completely disorganised: receipts for supplies were stored in a shoebox and appointments recorded in a personal diary, but she assumed that processing and filing on a computer were too difficult. When it came to preparing her tax return or tracking client hours LM knew that she was wasting precious time on paper-based methods but alternative methods seemed too daunting. It was only when a family member offered to explain how to use spreadsheets that she realised how straightforward it was. From then on, LM recorded her income and expenditure on her computer. This helped LM to reduce paper clutter and manage her business finances more effectively. It had been a lack of confidence rather than the level of difficulty which had held her back.

If you believe something is too difficult, probe a little deeper into the assumptions you're making about the task and about your own abilities. Is it really beyond your expertise? What skills would you need to learn and how could you acquire them? Let go of limiting beliefs, adopt a growth mindset and you'll be amazed at what you can accomplish.

It's way too big

It's always difficult for me to predict how each of my clients will perceive the scale of a challenge. A recently divorced professional can feel just as anxious about decluttering a one-room studio as an elderly couple might about downsizing from a five-bedroom family house to a smaller retirement flat. The perception of the size of a task is subjective, but if you feel that something is too big it can prevent you from making a start.

If you're deterred by the enormity of a task, here are some shrink-to-fit strategies that might help:

- **Be specific**
  A general idea can be intimidating but when it's reframed as a specific and measurable goal it becomes less daunting. Finding a job may seem like an insurmountable challenge but name the position you're after and the companies you'd like to work

for – define your aims more precisely – and it might change your perspective

- **Break it down**

  Instead of contemplating the task in its entirety, break it down into bite-sized chunks. Create a list of all the separate and distinct stages that you'll need to work through. Set micro-goals so that you can monitor progress. This strategy also helps to create a structure, which can be particularly useful for creative projects

  For example, when writing this book I listed all the different excuses and then set about fleshing out the book by taking it a chapter at a time. Without a clear framework and a step-by-step approach, this book would never have been written!

  Preparing for exams can also seem like a mammoth task but planning a study schedule and tackling it piecemeal is the most constructive strategy. The decision by the BBC Education Department to market their online revision resources as 'BBC Bite-Size' was inspired!

- **Focus on first, small steps**

  If it seems like an awfully long way from A to B don't think about your destination. Focus instead on taking the first steps, however small. So if you can't face sorting out all the paperwork on your desk, aim to deal with just one file. Don't worry if you start slow, the pace will probably pick up as you progress. Just remember that any movement which takes you in the right direction is movement worth celebrating. Children's author Louis Sachar says, 'Every time I start a new novel it seems like an impossible undertaking. If I tried to do too much too quickly, I would get lost and feel overwhelmed. I have to go slow and give things a chance to take form and grow'.[26] You might like to adopt this approach.

---

26 Louis Sachar, Author Spotlight, https://www.randomhouse.com/kids/catalog/author.pperl?authorid=26631&view=sml_sptlght

Fears

I don't know what I might uncover

Are you feeling stuck because taking a step forward feels like too much of a risk? This can lurk beneath the surface of many of the excuses discussed in this book.

Tackling paperwork, for example, can be a risky business because you never know what you might find or what you might discover you've lost. It can feel less stressful to leave the paper mountain untouched.

If your finances are disorganised or you're worried about debt, every letter that comes through the door can spark anxiety. Opening an envelope could mean encountering a reminder of your failure to meet deadlines and even a risk of financial penalties. But even if your funds are in the black, dealing with written correspondence can be intimidating. It may lead to unwelcome demands on your time or energy. Letters might include invitations that require a response or call for action. There's a risk that you'll be confronted by the need to make decisions!

The irony of course is that neglecting vital tasks for fear of what you might uncover increases the chances of other, possibly more serious risks. Delay a dental check-up because you're afraid of a filling and you're more likely to need costlier and more painful treatment in future. Ignore those brown envelopes labelled HMRC and you could discover that tax really can be taxing.

Take a deep breath and take that first step now

Take a deep breath and take that first step now, knowing that delaying it further will only increase, not reduce, the risk of uncovering bad news.

People might criticise me

In the fast-paced, interconnected world in which we live and work there are endless opportunities for others to comment on virtually every aspect of our lives. In a strange reversal of roles, schoolchildren can now post reports about teachers on Rate My Teacher. The National Health Service invites patients to write online reviews of GP practices, hospitals and clinics. And social media platforms such as Facebook and Twitter provide opportunities for anyone with a smartphone to express approval or disdain for anything or anyone at any time.

Journalist Owen Jones tweeted the following about his experience of social media:

> 'I wouldn't choose to walk every day into a room full of total strangers screaming mindless abuse and making up what I think and what my motives are, but in a sense, that's what I'm currently doing'[27]

No one enjoys negative feedback but is fear of criticism holding you up? Are you hesitating to launch a product or start a project because you worry about what people might say?

If you're launching a product or business and you're worried about online reviews, recent research for Reevoo suggests that there are advantages to less-than-perfect reviews.[28] 95% of readers revealed that they wouldn't trust a site which didn't have any bad reviews – they would assume the reviews were fabricated. So, ironically, reading criticism builds trust.

Poor feedback also gives business owners an opportunity to respond to customer complaints. Wouldn't you rather know what had gone wrong or how you had failed to live up to their expectations?

---

27 Owen Jones's Twitter ID is @owenjones84
28 Hannah Murray-Sykes, Can Good Reviews Be Bad for Business? https://blog.reevoo.com/good-reviews-bad-business

And when entrepreneurs or managers respond publicly to reviews, especially online, customers are impressed. Even if you can't solve the problem the fact that you are showing you care enhances your credibility.

Here's an example:

LT runs a printing company which produces branded merchandise for conferences. She was asked by a contact to print some stickers, however the printing didn't go according to plan. When the first batch was delivered to the client, LT received an email to say that the quality wasn't good enough. Whether the problem was due to human or technological error wasn't relevant to LT. What mattered most was that she reordered a new batch of stickers immediately, apologised to the client and let them know when the new stickers would be ready. The client had been disappointed with the initial product but was so impressed at the way LT handled the mistake that she didn't hesitate to recommend her to other local businesses.

Finally, remember that if you do get a bad review, you'll be in good company. Search on Amazon for reviews of The Hunger Games, one of the all-time best-selling books, and you'll see that 2% of 56,000 readers gave it a one star rating.

Getting a bad review online might be perceived as a

form of failure (see "I might fail" for more on that) and it can be hard to stomach if you're a perfectionist (see "I want it to be perfect"). But don't let it hold you back, it's part of our modern way of doing business.

The same principle could be applied to more traditional forms of feedback such as staff development or peer reviews. Instead of anticipating negativity, regard it as the start of a conversation with a trusted colleague, a chance to express concerns or clarify goals. And even if you encounter criticism, remember that it's an opportunity to address grievances, correct misunderstandings and resolve problems.

Now what if you're not a business owner and you're simply worried about other people (colleagues, friends, relatives) belittling your project or actions with sneery comments or negative reactions which could undermine your confidence? Even if you haven't yet experienced any opposition, the anticipation or fear that it might happen can get in your way. But try to let go of anxieties relating to things which haven't happened. Try to focus attention on what *is* rather than what might be. After all, the things you dread may never occur.

Try to let go of anxieties relating to things which haven't happened

And if they do happen, and people are less than

supportive of your plans or ideas, consider this: their reaction might be related to how they feel about themselves rather than anything you can control. They could be envious of your plans, your skills or what they perceive as your confidence. They could be struggling with personal issues which cause them to lash out at others. You can't control other people but you can control how you react to them. In this case it might be best not to react at all and simply continue on with your plans.

It's too risky

It's impossible to predict the outcome of every action but you can waste an awful lot of time trying to do so! And ruminating about risk can make it difficult to move forward.

If risk aversion is an issue for you the following questions might be helpful:

- What's at stake? Can you be absolutely sure?
- What is the worst possible outcome?
- What strategies and support do you have in place to deal with this?

Ultimately, the risk of inaction could be even greater than the chance of something going wrong if you have a go. Procrastination can carry a weighty price tag. Weigh up the longer term consequences of avoiding that task, decision or difficult conversation. If you don't summon up the courage to ask someone out on a date or talk to your boss about a promotion, you might miss out on life-changing opportunities.

You might miss out on life-changing opportunities

But even in the short term there are risks to holding back: living with the knowledge that you're stalling and that things could be different will fuel self-criticism and undermine your confidence and wellbeing. So take a chance, make a move and feel your confidence increase as things progress.

Responsibility

It's not my job

It's late in the evening and your children are fast asleep. As usual, the living-room floor is strewn with Lego and toy cars but you have no inclination to tidy up. Although in principle you'd love your home to be tidier, there's a grumbling resentment that stops you from tackling the chaos. Why do the kids make so much mess? Why doesn't your partner share the housework more equitably? Why is it always left to you to clear up? You feel irritated and demotivated.

Similar scenarios are played out daily in the workplace, particularly if roles and responsibilities become blurred. Imagine your boss asks you to complete a report for a colleague who can't meet a deadline. Or your team nominate you, for the umpteenth time, to write up the minutes of a meeting. It's hard to generate enthusiasm for tasks that you don't perceive to be part of your remit.

Step into a mental place of choice

If a feeling of resentment is blocking your productivity the key is to step into a mental place of choice. Recognise when and how you are actually exercising some degree of free will. This shifts the focus from extrinsic motivation (pleasing others or giving into pressure) to intrinsic motivation (finding purpose and meaning of one's own).

Ask yourself the following questions:

- Is this a one-off situation which you might just need to get over?
- Are there are perks to tackling this task? Will you learn anything from doing it, for example?

If so, you may want to tell yourself that you are going to choose to perform this task this time around.

However if this is part of a familiar pattern and taking on this task could set a precedent leading to further exploitation, you might find that learning to say 'No' effectively helpful. Regardless of its validity, the statement 'It's not my job' can come across as whingy and can make you seem small-minded, selfish and disloyal because you're putting your individual interests above that of the relationship, group or company. So it's important to say 'No' in the right way. In workshops entitled 'The Positive Power of No' I invite parents or professionals to practise strategies which enable them to develop more effective boundaries with family or colleagues and encourage them to find polite, simple and direct ways to communicate their reasons and concerns. You could do this by practising responses, such as:

- 'I'd like to help but can't right now'
- 'I'm happy to help with X' – set boundaries by naming a specific contribution
- 'Let's do it together' – share the load

If something really isn't your responsibility, work on taking control of the situation whilst remaining polite.

Only I can do this

Do you tend to assume control for every detail of a project such as planning a holiday? Do you find it difficult to trust others to carry out activities which meet your standards? Do you find it difficult to delegate? If you have answered yes to any of these questions and find yourself overwhelmed with too much on your plate, it's time to take stock.

Ask yourself what you can declutter from your to-do list. You might start by identifying what you want to hold onto: the tasks which would benefit from what my friend Rivka Caroline refers to as your 'unique brilliance'.[29] What do you do that others really can't replicate? If you're running a business you'll appreciate the importance of focusing time and energy on your key strengths. But the same is true for anyone keen to be productive.

Then get comfortable with delegation for your other tasks. There are many positive reasons for learning to delegate. First and foremost it enables you to lighten your load and concentrate time and energy on what you do best. By sharing responsibilities with others, you'll be issuing challenges which can empower and develop others. And by building a team you can develop and demonstrate leadership skills.

Get comfortable with delegation

Consider what kind of support is available and the cost. Depending on what you want to delegate, consider the pros and cons of engaging:

- Friends and family
- Sub-contractors
- Hired professionals
- Partnerships and collaborations

---

29 *Rivka Caroline, From Frazzled to Focused: The Ultimate Guide for Moms Who Want to Reclaim Their Time, Their Sanity and Their Lives, River Grove Books, 2013*

Remember that asking for help is not a sign of weakness; it takes courage to admit your own limitations and to approach others for assistance. So don't let insecurity stand in the way of delegation.

Asking for help is not a sign of weakness

There's more, however, to delegating than simply handing work to others. In order to get the maximum benefit, and to feel comfortable about doing it, here are some tips:

- **Recruit the right people**
  It may take time to locate and recruit suitable support but this is absolutely key to effective delegation. Don't take short cuts – research different options, check credentials, ask for references

- **Plan ahead and think strategically**
  Set short term goals but keep the bigger picture in mind. You might need to invest time training someone to work alongside you but once they can work more independently, you'll be able to delegate more to them in the future

- **Provide clear and detailed instructions**
  Ddon't expect others to read your mind or to anticipate what exactly needs to be done

- **Let go of the idea of perfection**
  No one else will do the job exactly like you and it may not be done to quite the same standard but sometimes good enough will be good enough. (See "I want it to be perfect" for more on this)

- **Maintain direct communication but don't micro-manage**
  Stay in touch and provide honest feedback but give others time and space to get on with the work

- **Express appreciation**
  This not only motivates others but also builds good working relationships

Learning to delegate is a vital life skill. It will help you to declutter a busy schedule and create time and energy for the activities you value most and which only you can do.

Someone else is holding me up

Is there anything in the world more frustrating than being held up by someone else's inaction? You can't plan the house move because solicitors/mortgage brokers/

estate agents are lingering over contracts. You'd like to send out invoices but need specific information from suppliers. The garage needs to be decluttered but your partner still hasn't moved the heavy boxes that they promised to shift last month.

When I run workshops in corporate settings on overcoming procrastination, I frequently hear staff complain about the inefficiency of colleagues, often more senior, because it has a direct impact on their own productivity: 'If I don't know when my boss will provide the content, I can't finish my presentation', 'I can't plan my annual leave and book my holiday until my company announces the date of our next conference'. These situations can be stressful, and waiting can breed feelings of passivity and powerlessness. It can, however, also be a convenient excuse for not getting things done!

If you find yourself playing the blame game here are some ideas to help you move things along:

- **Shift into a more proactive mode**
  Identify what you can do rather than dwelling on what you can't. Do you really need to be in full control of all the facts before you embark on your part of the project? Perhaps you could engage in some preliminary research, draft some initial plans/slides/designs while you wait for input? If you can't declutter the garage until your partner is available

to help, perhaps you can warm up by sorting out the garden shed on your own? Take the lead and initiate change rather than waiting for someone else

- **Challenge your own assumptions**
  Is it true that only your boss/colleague/partner can do the job that's holding you up? Could you enlist someone else to do it?

- **Communicate your request clearly and directly**
  Does your boss/colleague/partner understand the implications of their inaction? Perhaps if you explain without criticism, it might motivate them to prioritise the task that you need them to do

- **Stay positive and patient**
  Take the lead and display the behaviour that you'd like to see in others. Sometimes the traits we find most difficult to tolerate in others reflect traits we struggle to accept in ourselves. Before complaining about their procrastinating tendencies check whether there are other aspects of your work that you could be doing more efficiently yourself

Self-Beliefs

I'm too disorganised

If you've ever missed a flight or a deadline, lost your keys or forgotten to renew your car insurance you've probably berated yourself for being disorganised. And comparing yourself to others who appear to be more productive and organised may result in you feeling even worse. Why can't you be like the 'super mum' at the school-gates, the one who works flexible hours so that she can do the school run, who volunteers for the PTA and turns up to every fundraising event with homemade cupcakes? Or why are you staying late at the office yet again because you can't clear your desk while colleagues head off to the pub?

Shifting your mindset is the first step to shifting habits

People who perceive themselves as disorganised often assume that it's an innate weakness or even a moral failing, but the label can be self-perpetuating. My role as a professional organiser often involves helping clients to rid themselves of guilt, shame and judgement. Shifting your mindset is the first step to shifting habits.

The Institute for Challenging Disorganization in the US has conducted research into why some people are chronically disorganised.[30]

- Disorganisation which has persisted for many years
- A detrimental impact on quality of life
- Frequent (yet futile) efforts at self-help
- Low self-esteem and low expectations of change

Do any of these resonate with you? If they don't, then perhaps it's time to adjust your perception of just how disorganised you really are, and to ditch that self-perpetuating label?

The good news is that even if you do identify with these characteristics, you can still master time management and organising techniques. It may require more patience, persistence and support but the shift can happen. And if people with chronic disorganisation can shift debilitating habits, so can those with less severe challenges – you!

In my experience there are two basic elements to becoming more organised: creating systems and developing routines to maintain them.

For instance, you've heard the adage 'a place for everything and everything in its place'. It really is

---

30 The ICD Guide to Challenging Disorganization: For Professional Organizers, edited by Kate Varness, 2012

that simple, although it doesn't need to be taken to extremes. Allocating a place for household items promotes efficiency because you know where to find things and where to put them away when you've finished using them. There's no need to rack your brains looking for things or to waste time deciding where to store them. It also saves money because you don't have to replace things that you've lost.

But systems are only effective if they can be implemented continuously by you and your family or your team. That's why I encourage clients to adopt organising solutions that suit their home or office and their lifestyle. There's no point imposing systems that can't be maintained, so ensure that you adopt a system which works for you.

Developing routines is key to an organised schedule

This also applies to managing time: developing routines is key to an organised schedule. As As Benjamin Franklin wrote, 'Let all your things have their places; let each part of your business have its time'. Read more on this in the Time section of this book.

I'm too organised

Are you constantly compiling to-do lists but never actually get around to ticking things off? Are you obsessed with designing spreadsheets or overly-detailed project plans?

If you spend so much time and effort getting organised that you don't embark on doing the things that prompted you to get organised in the first place, you may have fallen into a common trap: focusing more on the apparatus than the activity.

Creating tools to boost productivity can be quite compelling. I often coach students who spend hours drawing up beautifully crafted revision aids: timetables featuring colour-coded checklists or flashcards that resemble small-scale works of art. It can be satisfying to design sophisticated resources but it would be more useful to actually utilise them.

The next time you find yourself fiddling with margin widths on a spreadsheet or adjusting fonts on a document, ask yourself whether presentation really warrants this amount of attention and whether it is actually helping to move you forward. Remember that creating tools for organising are a means to an end, not the end in itself.

I'm a procrastinator

At my 'I'll Do It Tomorrow' workshops I welcome the participants by asking them to raise their hand if they regard themselves as procrastinators. Most do, often with a nervous smile or laugh. Then I respond with some words of reassurance: 'You reserved a place in advance for this event and arranged to come. Some of you made complex plans with babysitters, coordinated lifts or checked public transport routes. The fact that you're here, on time and ready to take part suggests to me that you are *not* a procrastinator'. The people who would benefit most from my workshops, I joke, are the ones who didn't get around to booking a ticket.

But you think of yourself as a procrastinator? Is that a label that you have stuck on your own forehead, metaphorically speaking? Were you branded by parents, siblings, teachers or friends during childhood? Or is it an identity that you've assumed at a specific point in life such as while studying at university or working in a particular job?

Saying that you're a procrastinator isn't simply an act of description. It carries a great deal of self-judgement. So adopting the label can become part of the problem, rather than helping you find a solution.

A better approach is to focus on your behaviour rather than an identity. Yes, you have procrastinating tendencies – and some may be long standing and deeply ingrained but they don't permeate every area of your life. Your habits do not need to define who you are.

Your habits do not need to define who you are

Try to shift your perspective. Think about what you *do* accomplish every day rather than what you don't. Perhaps you take for granted the fact that you prepare breakfast, get your children dressed and take them to school every weekday morning? Maybe you underestimate the time management required to walk your dog every day? Chances are you've prioritised these activities and developed routines so that you and others can rely on. So give yourself credit for what you achieve. Take stock of routines that you've developed, especially those that involve other people.

Once you can admit that in certain areas of your life you are, in fact, quite productive, it will be easier to tackle the areas where there is scope for improvement.

I work well under pressure

One of the issues I frequently discuss with coaching clients is the role of deadlines. For some a deadline provides a useful framework: it helps to structure goals, measure progress and galvanise you into action. For others it can provide an excuse to postpone: why get started on that important study or work project when there's still plenty of time? See section "I still have plenty of time" for more on this.

Another reason for leaving things to the eleventh hour is the belief that you perform well when the clock is ticking. Maybe you savour the adrenalin rush? Or believe you find it easier to shut out distractions and focus?

But take a moment to think about this and be honest with yourself. Do you really believe that the work you produce during an all-night essay crisis is the most well-structured, thoughtful and insightful work you could produce? Is the email you wrote in the early hours of the morning to your boss likely to be the most coherent and constructive one? The harsh reality is that while time pressure might give the impression of boosting creative output, it saps energy and jeopardises performance.

According to Tom de Marco, expert on project management, 'People under pressure don't work better, they just work faster'.[31]

And aside from the quality of the work you're

---

31 Tom de Marco, Peopleware, Productive Projects and Teams, Addison Wesley, 2016 producing at the last moment ask yourself this: you may work well under pressure but how well do you *live* under pressure? What price are you paying in terms of stress? How does it impact your health, wellbeing and relationships? You might get away with an occasional last-minute marathon but the effects of stress are cumulative. Regularly working under pressure can take a serious toll, both physically and emotionally. How different could your life be if you learned to manage time more effectively?

You may work well under pressure but how well do you live under pressure?

This can be quite a thorny issue to tackle, especially among young adults and professionals, because working well under pressure can be misconstrued as a desirable skill. Prospective employers ask candidates in interview situations if they work well under pressure, but what they actually want to discover is whether the candidate is capable of making decisions in a rapidly-changing situation, can lead a team if someone drops out or can deal with an emergency. Their question is an opportunity for the candidate to demonstrate versatility, problem-solving skills and resilience – exploring the candidate's response to external factors and pressures beyond their control. This is quite different to working under pressure you've imposed on yourself by choosing to ignore or avoid thinking about deadlines.

So next time, before you make the statement that you work well under pressure, ask yourself if it's really true, and do you really need to? After all, just because you *can* do something doesn't mean you should.

I lack confidence

Finding ways to increase your personal confidence can make you more productive by enabling you to think more creatively, communicate more boldly and take more initiative. The following strategies could help:

- Think back to when you did something worthwhile at work and keep a visual reminder on your desk or on your phone. This could be a photo of an event that you've helped to organise or an email from a satisfied client. The point is to keep that memory alive. Owners of small businesses post testimonials on their websites in order to impress potential customers but in doing so also boost their own confidence

- Set micro-targets for success and monitor your own progress by daily stock-takes of communications or incidents, however minor, which demonstrate your competence. It can be hard to trust that you're doing a good job – or even a great job – without supporting evidence. So develop a habit of seeking out that evidence, actively looking for proof that you're on the right course

- Ask your line manager, colleagues or clients how you're doing. This doesn't need to be a formal review; just a few words of praise can reassure you that you're providing a good service or performing well. And if the feedback is less than excellent, treat it as useful feedback from which you can learn, not as criticism

Finally, remember that confidence is not an innate trait but rather a set of beliefs. It's possible to nurture and improve confidence. Don't aim for perfection – you can't always be 100% confident – but even small increases can help you to be more productive.

I'm easily distracted

If you read the blogs and biographies of inspiring people, the common theme is a high level of focus.

Success takes a combination of vision, drive and energy but one of the key ingredients of focused minds is the ability to manage distractions.

When I talk to coaching clients about distractions, conversations immediately turn to technology. How much time do you spend on your computer, phone or tablet? Do you notice how often you break off from your work or study to check emails or social media? Parents often complain that their son or daughter appears to be 'surgically attached' to their mobile phone. Students tell me that digital devices are a major source of distraction. But it's not only young adults who display addictive behaviour. A recent study found that 52% of adults checked their phone within fifteen minutes of waking up and 86% did so within an hour[32]. So if technology is your problem, you're not alone.

> One of the key ingredients of focused minds is the ability to manage distractions

It's worth noting however that inattention predates the internet. According to sociologist Frank Furedi, from

---

32 Rob Price, 1 in 3 people check their smartphones in the middle of the night, http://uk.businessinsider.com/1-in-3-people-check-smartphones-night-deloitte-study-2016-9

ancient times humans have grappled with distraction but what's changed is the way the problem is perceived. In previous centuries inattention was associated with indolence and perceived as a sign of moral weakness. Nowadays, in what he terms the Age of Distraction, it's regarded as 'normal' behaviour.[33]

But there are ways to improve your focus:

- **Control the culprits**
  Switch off your phone, or at least turn off notifications and sound. Put it in a drawer or bag so it's out of sight (and hopefully, out of mind). Perhaps give it to someone trustworthy with strict instructions not to return it until an agreed time

- **Monitor your mood**
  Chances are that you're more likely to be distracted when you're stressed, tired or bored. Take note of the times when your energy and concentration levels are highest and plan more complex or challenging tasks at those times of day

- **Doodle**
  If you're distracted during lectures or meetings,

---

33 Frank Furedi, The ages of distraction, http://www.frankfuredi.com/article/the_ages_of_distraction

studies now show that doodling can help.[34] Scribbling in the margins of notes or drawing abstract patterns not only improves focus; it also helps to boost memory, generate ideas and solve problems

- **Use fidget toys**
  The latest craze in schools and colleges is so-called 'self-regulation toys' to help concentration by keeping hands busy. Initially devised for students with ADHD or other special educational needs, they're becoming increasingly popular with teenagers and adults alike

- **Create purposeful playlists**
  If you come across interesting or useful podcasts, articles, blogs or videos, store them in a playlist, or bookmark them. When you're tempted to take a break from work or study, go to this list. If you have to take a break, at least you'll be doing something useful

---

34 Jackie Andrade, What does doodling do? Applied Cognitive Psychology, February 2009.
See also Rachel Smith, Drawing in Class, TEDXUFM, https://www.youtube.com/watch?v=3tJPeumHNLY

- **Harness technology**
  Instead of blaming devices for diverting attention, use them to control interruptions. Download timer apps that prevent you from accessing games or social media or limit usage for specific time frames

Whilst it may not be possible to completely ignore all distractions, learning to manage or reduce them can be very beneficial.

I can never finish anything

Do you get so caught up in a task that you lose sight of your goal? Perhaps you keep putting 'finishing touches' to a creative project but never actually finish it? Or you keep updating and editing an email to an old friend but never get around to sending it. You might perceive it as a work in progress but the reality is that you don't know where or how to stop. A creative process can be satisfying but if you're unable to complete the task you won't reap any benefit or experience any sense of accomplishment.

For some people the thrill of embarking on something new is far greater than the delight of completing it. Do you love brainstorming ideas and devising plans but find their implementation less fun?

Do you accumulate unfinished projects, things that you've abandoned after getting stuck?

So how can you be more productive when you don't know where, when or how to stop? Consider whether any of these factors relate to you:

- **Perfectionism**
  You're never satisfied that what you've produced is good enough. But it doesn't need to be perfect, it often just needs to be done. See "I want it to be perfect" for advice on this

- **Curiosity**
  You're genuinely fascinated by whatever you're learning and keen to fully explore the subject before you switch to another activity. But just because you complete a specific project doesn't mean that you can't investigate it further in future

- **Enjoyment**
  Put bluntly, the more fun you're having with a task, the less incentive there is to finish it! But again, finish this task and you can move on to another you'll enjoy just as much

- **Lack of clarity**
  If you're not absolutely sure of the parameters

how will you know when a project is finished? Mapping out your goals clearly and checking that you understand the requirements and expectations of others will help you to avoid this trap

- **Anxiety**
  You're worried about the outcome or the feedback you'll receive so you avoid completing things or avoid giving others the chance to comment. Sooner or later you'll have to face the music so why delay the inevitable? And the longer you leave it, the more you're likely to worry

- **Apprehension**
  You don't where the project will lead and what changes this might entail. Fear of success can be just as powerful as fear of failure but I invite you to trust in yourself and in your ability to cope with whatever the future holds

Some of the other excuses addressed in this book can be just as relevant to not finishing as they are to not getting started, so take a look at other sections too.

Keep going, finish the project, congratulate yourself and make space to move on to something equally or more satisfying and engaging.

Results

I want it to be perfect

'Perfect' must be the most over-used marketing buzzword of our times. Take a quick glance through any newspaper or magazine and you'll find adverts for 'perfect' sofas or furnishings, dating websites enticing you to search for a 'perfect partner' recruitment firms claiming to offer 'perfect jobs' and recipes for 'perfect' pies or pizzas. But the pursuit of perfection is completely pointless. Neither your sofa, your partner, nor your job need be perfect – they just need to suit you. And as for pastry goods, I'll settle for nutritious and delicious.

There's nothing wrong with wanting to do your best but the myth of perfection fuels insecurities which in turn undermine motivation. What's the point of attempting something if you can't do it perfectly?

Rivka Caroline, author of From Frazzled to Focused, refers to procrastination and perfectionism as 'evil twins'. She captures brilliantly the difficulties we create for ourselves by setting impossible standards:

> 'Living life with perfectionist standards is the emotional equivalent of choosing to walk

> between two buildings on a tightrope, rather than simply walking across the street. It's dangerous, highly risky, and fraught with anxiety for you and all those around you'[35]

In my study skills coaching I've worked with several teenagers who were high achievers but struggled with time management due to perfectionism. They put themselves under immense pressure not only to succeed in homework or exams, but to gain full marks. These students admit that they are far more critical of themselves than of anyone else in their life. And they tend to view things in simplistic terms: success is an all or nothing concept.

Can you identify with this? If the idea of perfection causes you to postpone making a start on tasks, or if worrying about every detail and having impossibly high standards results in slow progress, ask yourself this simple question: why aim for perfection when excellent will do?

You could actually lower the bar even further. Acknowledge that there are times when mediocrity may be sufficient. In fact, you could even argue that in certain situations, if a job's worth doing, it's worth

---

35 Rivka Caroline, From Frazzled to Focused: The Ultimate Guide for Moms Who Want to Reclaim Their Time, Their Sanity and Their Lives, River Grove Books, 2013

doing badly! If you're struggling with a particular piece of work there's no point in trying to perfect it. For instance, handing in a piece of work which scores a low mark can alert your tutor or teacher to any gaps in your understanding. It might not be an ideal solution but rather than agonising about perfection, just do your best and finish the task.

It doesn't need to be perfect: it just needs to be done

Context is clearly key. But the antidote to perfectionism is to learn to distinguish between when 100% is required and when it isn't. Most of the time I'm sure you'll find that it doesn't need to be perfect: it just needs to be done.

I can't imagine it done

Does your heart sink at the thought of sorting out the loft? Is it so full of junk that you've accumulated for years that you can't imagine what decluttering would deliver? Or do you get palpitations when you see an email from your tutor or boss about a pending research project? You've never written a 30,000-word report nor have you read one by anyone else so you don't really know what it should look like. When faced with a major project, one of the challenges can be simply to imagine it done.

How can you start something if you can't imagine its completion? You might feel that you need to see the finishing line before you leave the starting block – but perhaps you don't?

If you can't imagine a clear loft, a dissertation that's ready to submit or a report ready to share with colleagues, this is how to create a vision:

- **First steps**
  Close your eyes and picture yourself climbing up a ladder to open the loft, for example, or writing the opening paragraph of an essay. Imagine the anticipation

- **Into your stride**
  Now witness yourself fully engaged in the task, packing up bags in the loft or tapping away at the keyboard while writing your assignment. Notice the progress that you're making

- **Result!**
  This can be the most challenging image but be bold. It may require a stretch of the imagination to picture the final product. Dare to dream but don't

worry about trying to predict what exactly the result will look like

- **Impact**
  Don't focus on the material result; imagine what difference it will make to your life and try to connect with the positive emotions that you'll experience. Imagine the satisfaction of finding your camping gear in the loft quickly and easily. Visualise yourself taking part in a graduation ceremony while your family watch with pride

A few words of warning:

- Don't confuse visualisation with fantasy. Keep it real
- There's no need to predict an exact outcome. Don't worry if you don't yet know what kind of storage you'd like to install in the loft or what type of font you'll use for your dissertation
- Be prepared to encounter cynicism or self-doubt. When you take a leap forward, even in your imagination, it can be scary. But don't be daunted, dare to dream
- Once you have a vision it's likely to be easier to make a start.

I might fail

This fear is closely related to perfectionism but it's not only perfectionists who find themselves paralysed or stuck for fear of failing.

The word 'failure' conjures up negative emotions such as shame, embarrassment and humiliation. If you think of events in your life which you associate with failure you might also recall having physical sensations such as blushing, sweaty palms or shallow breathing.

But as educators and parents know, failing is vital to learning. Watch a toddler learning to walk – they fall, again and again, but pull themselves up and persevere until they master the art.

It's only by reframing our attitudes to failure that we can overcome inhibitions and paralysis. Thomas Edison, holder of more than 1093 patents including the light bulb, paved the way for viewing failure in positive terms: 'I have not failed. I've just found 10,000 ways that won't work'. Edison's words and deeds also highlight the importance of persistence: 'The most certain way to succeed is always to try just one more time'.

One of the ways in which I try to help students feel more positively about failure is to point out that those who are awarded lower grades for essays at the beginning of a course will improve more than other students. If they are willing to learn from feedback they will gain more than students whose essays are brilliant from the outset.

I also run workshops for small business owners on learning from mistakes where I invite participants to share lessons gained from messing up. These could be errors of judgement such as poor investments or mistakes such as miscalculating an invoice. Many find it difficult to talk about these issues as they are not accustomed to revealing their vulnerabilities.

If you are hesitating to do something because you're afraid you might fail, what can you do to reduce your anxiety?

Distinguish between outcome and identity

It's actually not usually the act of failing that we dread, but other people's responses to it. How would you feel about applying for a job if you knew that nobody among your social or professional circles would ever discover the outcome? Are your concerns about the opinions of others getting in your way? You might want to read "People might criticise me".

But what's most important is to distinguish between outcome and identity. Losing a sports tournament or presenting an unsuccessful funding bid can be disappointing. But failing in an endeavour doesn't make you a failure.

Some Final Thoughts

I hope that this book has provided food for thought and that it has motivated you to look afresh at the obstacles which you may be putting in your own way. You may have found some of the questions challenging but I hope that in those challenges you found some new ideas and inspiration.

I've included the excuses I've heard most frequently from my coaching clients over the years but the list isn't exhaustive. If your repertoire includes other excuses, please do get in touch and let me know.

While I've encouraged you to explore excuses I haven't suggested delving deeper into explanations. You haven't been asked, for example, to ponder whether habits stem from childhood or schooling, or whether they reflect tensions within past or current relationships. As a social scientist I'm fascinated by such theories. But as a coach, eager to motivate and mobilise clients to action, I'm more inclined to go with my grandmother's maxim: '"Why" is a crooked letter'. Think about what happens when someone asks you a question that starts with the word 'Why'. My hunch is that it takes you into your head but analysis doesn't get you moving. On the contrary, thinking about *why* you procrastinate might be yet another great excuse for not getting on with important tasks.

As a result, the emphasis of this book has been on helping you to find solutions rather than sources.

If you're feeling stuck, the way forward will often be found in your answers to these questions:

- **What** needs to be done? Identify positive goals and practical challenges
- **Who** needs to do it? Outline roles and responsibilities
- **How** does it need to be done? Define standards and choose methods
- **When** does it need to be done? Decide on timing, make plans and set priorities

We can't change all the circumstances of our lives but we can change the conversations that we have with others, and with ourselves. The aim of this book is to help you to do that. Be kind to yourself and let go of self-judgement. Open your mind to fresh perspectives and new possibilities. Try out some of the strategies I've suggested or adapt them to suit your own particular needs. As a result you'll start to make choices, develop confidence and feel less stressed. Most importantly you'll learn to make time for what you value most.

Learn to make time for what you value most

The result will be improved time management and productivity which in turn will result in more confidence, less stress, more time doing the things you most enjoy and a feeling of being more in control. Being more productive will enhance all areas of your life.

So, if you're eager to be more productive, start by listening to your excuses. Excuses are simply stories waiting to be retold.

Acknowledgements

First and foremost, I'd like to thank my parents, Mark and Naomi Pope and my brother Jonathan for championing me throughout life's ups and downs. Huge love and thanks also to Amitai and Elisheva who inspire me every single day.

Much gratitude to Joanne Henson, editor extraordinaire, for inviting me to write this book and for providing such professional support throughout the process. Thanks to Twitter for introducing us.

Close friends have helped me to overcome my own procrastination at key points. Thank you, especially, to Rivka Caroline, Ronit Knoble, Carolyn Spinks, Marcia Plumb, and Nicole Robinson for your love and laughter. Thank you also to Michael Diamond for tracking down elusive references.

I'd also like to express appreciation to both of my professional communities for providing so many opportunities for positive and productive conversations: the co-active coaching community, especially Corrina Gordon-Barnes, and APDO Association of Professional Declutterers & Organisers, especially Ingrid Jansen, Lesley Spellman and Clare Parrack. A shout-out too to networking buddies of Athena Central London, Buzzing Women, Laurel Leaf, and the NAGs.

Last but not least, I'd like to thank all of the students I've taught and the clients I've coached over the last three decades. Without you this book wouldn't have happened.

About the Author

Juliet Landau-Pope MA (Oxon), PGCertAP, CPCC, FHEA is a certified coach, professional organiser and study skills expert in London. An Oxford graduate, she has more than 25 years' experience of working in adult education as a university lecturer, researcher, editor, mentor, coach and consultant.

In 2008 she founded JLP Coach to provide a portfolio of services including practical decluttering and study skills coaching for adults and teenagers. She also leads innovative training in community and corporate settings to improve organising and time management.

In addition to running her own business, Juliet volunteers as a board member (head of training) for APDO Association of Professional Declutterers & Organisers.

Find out more at:

www.jlpcoach.com
Email: juliet@jlpcoach.com
Facebook: www.facebook.com/declutter
Twitter: @jlpcoach
Instagram: @jlpcoach

Index

Also in this series

What's Your Excuse for not Eating Healthily?

Joanne Henson

Overcome your excuses and eat well to look good and feel great

Do you wish you could eat more healthily and improve the way you look and feel, but find that all too often life gets in the way? Do you regularly embark on healthy eating plans or diets but find that you just can't stick with them? Then this is the book for you.

This isn't another diet book. Instead it's a look at the things which have tripped you up in the past and offers advice, ideas and inspiration to help you overcome those things this time around.

No willpower? Hate healthy food? Got no time to cook? Crave sugary snacks? Overcome all of these excuses and many more. Change your eating habits and relationship with food *for good*.

Paperback – ISBN 978-0-9933388-2-3

e-book – ISBN 978-0-9933388-3-0

Also in this series

What's Your Excuse for not Being Better With Money?

Jo Thresher

Overcome your excuses and get to grips with your personal finances

Do you wish you could be savvier with money but find it too daunting? Do you wish you were more in control of your finances but find yourself avoiding taking action? Then this is the book for you.

Personal finance expert Jo Thresher takes a look at all of the reasons you might give for not getting to grips with your money, and offers advice, ideas and inspiration to help you change that.

No time to get organised? Scared to look at your bank statement? Think you're a shopaholic? Not money minded? Overcome all of these excuses and many more. Improve your relationship with your cash and feel more secure, more relaxed and more in control.

Paperback – ISBN 978-0-9956052-0-6
e-book – ISBN 978-0-9956052-1-3

Also in this series

What's Your Excuse for not Living a Life You Love?

Monica Castenetto

Overcome your excuses and lead a happier, more fulfilling life

Are you stuck in a life you don't love? Have you reached a point where your life doesn't feel right for you anymore? Then this book is for you.

This is not yet another self-help book claiming to reveal the secret to permanent happiness. Instead, it helps you to tackle the things which have been holding you back and gives ideas, advice and inspiration to help you move on to a better life.

Don't know what you want? Scared of failure? Hate change? Worried about what others might think? This book will help you overcome all of your excuses and give you the motivation you need to change your life.

Paperback – ISBN 978-0-9933388-4-7

e-book – ISBN 978-0-9933388-5-4

Also in this series

What's Your Excuse for not Loving Your Job?

Amanda Cullen

Overcome your excuses and change the way you feel about your work

Do you have a job which you're not enjoying as much as you know you should? Do you dread Mondays, spend your free time worrying about your work or feel undervalued by your boss or colleagues? If so, this book is for you.

In this supportive and motivational book Amanda Cullen takes a look at the wide variety of excuses we use which keep us stuck and unhappy in our work. She offers ideas and advice on how to tackle issues so that you can take control, make the necessary changes and transform your working life.

Don't like your colleagues? Spend too long in the office? Not confident in your skills? Or just plain bored? Overcome all of these and many more, and learn how to love your job.

Paperback – ISBN 978-0-9933388-6-1
e-book – ISBN 978-0-9933388-7-8

Also in this series

What's Your Excuse for not Getting Fit?

Joanne Henson

Overcome your excuses and get active, healthy and happy

Do you want to be fit, lean and healthy, but find that all too often life gets in the way? Do you own a gym membership you don't use, or take up running every January only to give up in February? Then this is the book for you.

This is not yet another get-fit-quick program. It's a look at the things which have prevented you in the past from becoming the fit, active person you've always wanted to be, and a source of advice, inspiration and ideas to help you overcome those things this time around. Change your habits and attitude to exercise for good.

Too tired? Lacking motivation? Bored by exercise? You won't be after reading this book!

Paperback – ISBN 978-0-9933388-0-9

e-book – ISBN 978-0-9933388-1-6

Also in this series

What's Your Excuse for not Being More Confident?

Charlotta Hughes

Overcome your excuses, increase your confidence, unleash your potential

Do you feel you could achieve much more in life if only you had more confidence? Do you know you'd be happier if you were braver, or had more self-belief? Then this is the book for you.

In this supportive and motivational book former Life Coach of the Year Charlotta Hughes takes a look at all of the ways in which we hold ourselves back and avoid expanding our horizons and she offers advice, ideas and inspiration to help change things.

Scared of failure? Feel unappreciated? Hate change? Worried about what others might think? This book will help you overcome all of your excuses and give you the motivation you need to change the way you feel about yourself.

Paperback – ISBN 978-0-9933388-8-5
e-book – ISBN 978-0-9933388-9-2